I would like to thank the editors of the following journals in which the poems listed have appeared.

14 x 14: "The Mother Ship;" "Post Card"
American Arts Quarterly: "Sculpture"
Angle: "Café Le Vieux Montmartre;", "On the Beginning of Constant Memory"
Antiphon: "The Dream of Art"
Autumn Sky: "Kids on Bikes"
Chimaera: "Oak Park"
Ep;phany: "Tompkins Square;" "Caprichos"
E-Verse Radio: "Camp Allamuchy"
The Flea: "Sticking Point;" "Triduum;" "…wednesday"
Great Weather for Media 2013 Anthology: "Star Trek"
Lavender Review: "Recital;" "Lorelei"
Light Quarterly: "The Princeton Lab"
The Literary Bohemian: "Cologne"
Loch Raven Review: "Green Line to Lechmere"
Measure: "Under Glass;" "Sappho's Letter to Sophie"
The Raintown Review: "Belém"
Shit Creek Review: "Spanish Mustangs"
Soundzine: "The Marquis;" "Watching Women and Dogs On the Campo S. Maria Mater Domini"
Unsplendid: "Dead Catfish;" "Ungemalte Bilder"
We Are Kin: "My Fisherman's Sweater;" "Chimaera"

Thanks to Cally Conan-Davies, Jeff Holt, and Susan de Sola Rodstein for their advice and support. Thanks to the poets and critics of the Eratosphere critique board who have spent time with every poem in this collection. And thanks to Alyssa Kratsch for her keen eye at the lake.

Much gratitude to Michele Arboit, my editorial consultant, who saved me once again.

Thanks to Ernest Hilbert, R. Nemo Hill, and Rose Kelleher for their kind words.

And thanks to Elizabeth and Robert Murphy of Dos Madres Press for their confidence in my work and for their care in creating beautiful books.

Thanks and love always to my wife Maureen, and to my daughters Emily, Marguerite, and Lydia.

March 17, 2013

Front Cover:
Jonnie Pangyarihan, *Hamlet*, 2013
Oil on plastic card, 3.5" x 2.25"
From a series of portraits and skulls
painted on New York City subway fare cards

Frontispiece:
Neil Holmes, *The Common Calisthenics*, 2013
Ink and pencil on paper, 8" x 5"

Back Cover:
Todd Groesbeck, *Portrait of Rick Mullin*, 2011
Oil on linen, 16" x 13"
Collection of Steven Phillips and Dennis Keener

To the Memory of Paul Christian Stevens

*At the round earth's imagined corners, blow
Your trumpets, Angels, and arise, arise…*
—John Donne

Table of Contents

On Bloomfield / 1

1. ROSES FROM THE GAS STATION

Recital / 5
Sticking Point / 6
The Mother Ship / 7
Star Trek / 8
Triduum / 9
John Paul I / 10
My Fisherman's Sweater / 12
Camp Allamuchy / 13
Clouds / 14
The Tick Tock Diner / 15
…wednesday / 16
Chimaera / 17

2. THE FALLING RIDE

Oak Park / 21
Spanish Mustangs / 22
Green Line to Lechmere / 23
Tompkins Square / 24
The Marquis / 25
Post Card / 26
Sir Toby / 27
Watching Women And Dogs
    On the Campo S. Maria Mater Domini / 28
Caprichos / 29
Descansos Negras / 30
Café Le Vieux Montmartre / 31
Belém / 32

3. BEYOND THE GLANCING MOMENT

On the Beginning of Constant Memory / 39
The Dream of Art / 41
Just Friends / 42
Kids on Bikes / 43
Sculpture / 44
Dead Catfish / 45
Ungemalte Bilder / 47
Cologne / 48
Sappho's Letter to Sophie / 49
Zuiderkerk / 50
Rise / 51

4. THE BIG MONOPOLY

If What You Want is Fire / 57
The Postmodern Prometheus / 58
Permanent Lunch / 59
The Princeton Lab / 60
Under Glass / 61
Glitch / 62
Wheatfield with Crows / 63
In the Killer's Studio / 64
Chance / 65
Landing / 66
Lorelei / 67
The Strand / 68

On Bloomfield

Our beards are soft and gray as morning ash
endowed with parables and cigarettes.
Our coats, a vagary of petty cash,
describe the button holes in safety nets.
And if this station cracks beneath our boots,
the cold, erasing rain may knit us suits.

— *1* —

ROSES FROM THE GAS STATION

Recital

One cloud like an adamant balloon ship
came in over Branchport, scudding toward
the bluff, a spacious blue-gray change of weather.

It sprinkled on the Esperanza Mansion,
challenging the map of lily fronds
that mirrored in the lake all afternoon
like Queen Anne's lace. A scow that rolled to cover
half the sky with something like a welcome
dread advanced as I stood in recital
underneath a silver maple on the lawn.

"Three perfect days," she'd sighed and sipped her wine
before abandoning her wicker throne
dead-center on the lofting grass to take a nap
above the tree where I had come to read aloud.

Keuka Lake, August 8, 2012

Sticking Point

At 50 I am likely to arrive
with roses from the gas station, in need
of better shoes, a less frenetic haircut.
With a smile just barely managing
to hold the road. But here's the sticking point—
a destination. Someone at a real
concrete address to take delivery.
The county ledger tells you I'm a fool.
And when I come into a certain green
suburban arrondissement, rolling fast
with grade school children on an asphalt strip
along the Watchung ridge, a little girl
drops everything. She stands and looks
at me. She makes me stop the car
so she can run up to the driver's side
and rap the glass with hopping urgent news.
There's paperwork downtown. Municipal
directories. A letter with my name
upon a table. Here's another thing—
the siren echo as the street games end.
And, then, that jagged fire in the trees.

The Mother Ship

These stars that matter to the older brother
that I never had and to the older
sister who would not eclipse my mother
pool their energy as nights grow colder.

And these streets that end in parking lots
or wind on tracks beneath the crystal towers
tie their halide shadows into knots.
I have been navigating these for hours.

All is lost. Or somewhat nonexistent.
And it doesn't matter if I cry
to every Mother that I meet. Persistent
pain is like a window in the sky,

and I, the fallen child, the pioneer
deployed beneath this cut glass chandelier.

Star Trek

For Birdie

*Like it or not, we are probably trapped in our solar system
for a long, long time.*
Adam Frank

I know a woman in New Mexico
whose two young sons live mostly in between
the stars, exploring in a theater
of rolling planets, traveling at a speed
that doesn't register in time and space.
Their map is coloring an evening sky
that promises to tell the earth a story
in a scheme of light, the Beam of Lorelei,
a blessing from the mountain's Vulcan hand.
She hears their voices on a muted channel
in the hard-won silence of the porch at night.
A fever line divides her cobalt screen.
I know a woman in New Mexico
whose boys are simply there, between the stars.

Triduum

He said she looked at peace the second day,
Good Friday, but I saw her Thursday night,
her intubated body as it lay
deflated where the seven-hour fight
to keep her breathing mercifully stopped.

They'd pounded her so hard and for so long
she looked assaulted, like a fighter dropped
in extra rounds. My sister-in-law, strong
enough to mix with Lupus thirty years,
surrounded by her family, gave in.

On Easter Sunday, after several beers,
her brother, who'd gone back, gave us the spin.
But I'd seen her Irish brothers in her face.
The stony aura. That pugnacious grace.

John Paul I

For Michelle Brunetti

i saw you from your balcony window
and you were standing there waving at everybody
                                         Patti Smith

I can't retrieve the temporary pontiff's
face beyond that pink filet of haunted
newsprint in a miter. Substantive.
Formidable, but blank within a gilt
display. Torn out, the image was (what killed
him?) from the Sunday magazine. The milk

of Christ's beneficence kept burbling on
his smock, and draped upon the paragon
was lingerie! The pope was dead and gone
in just a month and a memorial
came cobbled to my dormitory. All
irreverence and mock theatricals,

sophomoric sculpture with the plastic flowers
from the coffee table. Gothic horrors.
Mary Godwin Shelley kept the hours,
it seemed, in chthonic tights and black brassiere.
The dance of Salome in veils was there,
where Strickland crammed biology. His sneer

betrayed him. Prophylactic irony
prevailed, a filter on the Holy See.
That famous smile does not come back to me
and thus I tend to substitute my father's
heavy features—But there's holy water
on the plastic flowers. Sons and daughters

frolic in the dormitory lobby
and, to tell the truth, we're kind of sorry
that a namesake and successor, holy
Karol, is in place. From what we saw,
a jutting smile across a Popeye's jaw,
there'd be no frills or flowers anymore.

My Fisherman's Sweater

The populace, attired in charcoal gray,
communicating sotto voce, plies
its ashen paths and paving stones today.
On sidewalks, pushing through the subway stiles,
a line of strangers, nondescript, performs
the common calisthenics. Everywhere
you look you see the urban uniforms,
deliberate obsidian, austere.
I, too, am cloaked in standard-issue black,
unpersonned in my scarf and coat and cap.
But you'd know where to send the body back,
were I to fall or fail to mind the gap.
One layer down, a cabled map is knit.
I found it after thirty years. It fit.

Camp Allamuchy

Salvo Louis—how he got that name
I can't recall—kept mostly to himself.
He stayed all summer with "Provisional,"
the weekly pick-up troop for boys who came
alone. He was obsessed with Steppenwolf.
He had a shoebox of cassettes, and all
he ever talked about, besides the group,
was how his fellow campers for the week
missed out on "primo shit" the week before.
He didn't make a lot of friends. Our troop,
which always had a campsite by the lake
the second week of August, would ignore
the "bastards" from Provisional. "The hoods."
But I knew who played *Monster* in the woods.

CLOUDS

His brother had a recipe for clouds,
but that was more a formula for magic
than for chemistry, a kind of tragic
folding of ingredients as shrouds
of cumuli advanced outside the lab,
above the kitchen where he couldn't see
and wouldn't have been able to decree
that all of heaven is a cake to grab
and carry in a shoebox to his room
where he could sleep on it and tell his friends
about the view, the colors from inside
as he gazed out from where the cloud line ends
or down into the bowl of murky gloom
he stirred, refrigerated, spooned, and fried.

THE TICK TOCK DINER

The Tick Tock Diner shines before a highway
graveyard, channeling the neon heyday
of aluminum, a phantom restaurant,
a dead man's foggy memory, a taunt
and beacon to the drivers on Route 3.
It faces off the old drug factory,
electric, bleeding red and blue into
the rain-wet lanes, *"Eat Heavy"* cutting through
the gaseous glare, a ring around the clock
and siren call, *pull over* (tick) *pull over* (tock)

pull over past the hour-rate motels
that glimmer in the watercolor swells
of tunnel traffic early Sunday morning.
Put your blinker on, sufficient warning
to the Turnpike ramp where tractor-trailers
rumble in the mist like drunken sailors,
shift and hydroplane. And if you listen
through the splashing gears that grind and glisten
you can hear that Russian waitress sigh.
Pull over while there's time. Pull over. Try.

...Wednesday

Having nearly snuffed it in a sitting
and now sitting through a four-day hack,
wanting only to be on my back
and staring at the ceiling, it is fitting
I convey my Wednesday reverie
to anyone who cares enough to hear:
Tequila's made of bigger stuff than beer.
That's all I have for now (apostrophe)
except how, with the smokes that rolled my binge
into an unaccustomed nimbus, I
may well have upped the pain and suffering
with so much else, *sólo un imbécil*,
no longer hanging on his so-called hinge,
who, now he's off it, knows no buffering.

Chimaera

Shadow sprite, a revenant bottom feeder,
spookfish, ratfish, rabbitfish, enigmata,
glides a mirror drone in the sun-comb strata,
hydrocephalic

catman, sitting pretty in AquaEgypt,
curling sand, exquisite on stone oasis
tepid green, a god in the amber hour,
elephant, flounder.

—2—

THE FALLING RIDE

Oak Park

I drove alone through Oak Park, Illinois,
with something vague and urgent on my mind.
The sun was setting. First I saw the boy
who scampered down a shingled roof. Behind
the house a row of hemlocks swayed in waves.
Next door I saw a girl who step-danced fast
from gable down to gutter. *She behaves
in miracles*, I thought as I drove past.

Preoccupied, a little shocked (and dreaming
at the wheel), I couldn't help them down.
I didn't stop the car. I heard no screaming
parent as I drove across a town
of barefoot infant acrobats on roofs
of slate with oak leaves saddled in the grooves.

Spanish Mustangs

For Laura Meschio

The horses came while we were at the beach
and rummaged through our garbage cans like rats—
enormous, pregnant rats with dreadlocks, each
a sunspot on the intercoastal flats,
a blind spot to the hapless lumber truck
or S.U.V. The legendary breed
appeared and disappeared today. Our luck.
It slipped us, filly, foal and woolly steed,
to shift beyond the pastel afternoon
behind the *Brew Thru* and development.
To hoof the waterline of the lagoon
where sunset casts the due envelopment
of twilight on imaginary streams
that cut across the white sand of our dreams.

Corolla, North Carolina,
August, 1994

Green Line to Lechmere

Getting on the subway here at 6:00 a.m.
I come upon a lighted hall of refugees.
A dormitory. Everything is quiet, grim,
the galley soft and gray with morning effigies.
I interrupt their sleep. A head might rise and fall
among the others as I hang beside the door
uncertain of my destination. Here I call
on numbers, an address, improbable before
these somnolescent passengers, their hair anointed
with the oils of their familiarity
as shoulder-pressed-to-shoulder in their pre-appointed
space they burrow to a regularity
of polyester coats and dirty woolen shrouds.
How passing strange to brush a suit into these clouds.

Boston, April 26, 2012

Tompkins Square

For Ray Pospisil

The park is outlined in the evergreen
eviction of a finished holiday,
epiphanies and parties gone the way
of decimated Christmas trees that lean
on curbs outside each brownstone residence.
A landscape from the takedown of the '80s.
Engraved above a pistol-black Mercedes:
Faith, Hope, Charity and Temperance.

But there are less ironic epilogues
to crown this January fountainhead
where flipping skateboards crack the atmosphere
like piles of iron ferrying the dead.
Where lovely, upscale couples with their dogs
boot needles at the dark door of the year.

New York City,
January 10, 2010

The Marquis

Night, 22nd floor

I wrote about you once when I was green,
a stringer for that business magazine
that covered energy. Remember me,
O San Francisco Marriott Marquis?
I interviewed your H-VAC engineers…
well, I guess it's more than 20 years
since PR mailed that color photograph.
The caption went on for a paragraph,
and I was glad to get you on the cover.
I even sent a copy to my mother.

Your scalloped atrium came just in time
to show the world how you make "earthquake" rhyme
with "cakewalk". Turquoise mirror to the sky,
a wing of ostentatious glitz on high,
you came up short of Transamerica—
your gift was more of esoterica
on Mission Street. An icon you are not.
But I was all about your "cold" and "hot"
and how your automation didn't flinch.
And I was getting paid per column inch.

You looked ridiculous and I felt cheap
and used. And now, I cannot get to sleep.
The off-white noise of your mechanic guts
keeps whirring in the dark—those gears and struts
I puffed for Honeywell and Carrier.
I was an all-too-willing terrier,
and now I suffer in a high rise hell.
I'm gray and anxious. Look at me, hotel!—
an old reporter shanghaied in a vault
that totters, still, on an enormous fault.

San Francisco Marriott Marquis, February 14, 2010

Post Card

My love, the clanging cable car on Hyde
was good enough to break the leaden spell
that folded me in fog. The falling ride
and hint of burning elevator smell
delighted me. I felt the weight of light,
the payload of a switchyard cabernet.
Into the lustrous loneliness of night
I rang up from the drone of lonely day.
It dangled by apartments till the chime
announced our progress in the rich and blighted
streets of twisted asphodel and thyme.
The brakeman dropped. A love song was recited.
And as the moon rode over Lombard Street,
I swung up from the sideboard to a seat.

San Francisco, November 11, 2009

Sir Toby

(with apologies to Laurence Sterne)

On Fleet Street, where the scribblers eat their lunch
and gangs of black-clad punks come up the stairs,
where *shoosh*!-ing Clockwork Orange chants meet Punch
and Judy grins, the crockwork Toby stares.
His shop-glass fronts a clash of gawky youth
and down-coat tourists from the colonies,
a dustup at the Underground, a tooth-
and-nail outside the bloody Cheshire Cheese.

A souvenir. The old cigar shop Whig
and Tricorn, pipe held tight to potted pouch.
Shall he not take his ease? His pint of swig?
Must *he* engage should "Rule Britannia" slouch
toward "*Anarchy-y-y*"? The Cock & Bull attest:
Men tire themselves in the pursuit of rest.

London, January, 1979

Watching Women and Dogs
on the Campo S. Maria Mater Domini

And yet another thin-dark beauty dressed
for summer with an English pit bull—yes,
I ogle, follow sunlit cotton lines
from shoulder down to thigh. I watch her slap
the white dog's flank, imagining her breasts
so olive-firm, such ripe commodities.

I'm slumped and drinking something red and sweet
decanted from the ancient plastic vats
beneath the register. It's fine, I guess.

And at the table next to me a woman,
lobster-baked, a Campo veteran
with clamshell rings (she's seen a war or two)
has closed her eyes. She's very beautiful.

Venice, June 30, 2007

Caprichos

I

Through the veins of light in the gothic quarter,
under stone in desolate La Ribera,
I advance, but not as a guided pilgrim
doggedly seeking

God in Oz apartments or climbing stairs through
dry cement Utopia. Shadow-silver
dreams, the Spanish dance of a Goya etching,
carry me forward.

II

Acid black, the blood of this city seeks a
common level, splashing at dirty ankles.
Civil war graffiti and worm-rut doorways
decorate alleys

calling forth the conical caps and Roman
juries, ghosts and vaporous ruminations.
Undigested tapas or bad sangria.
Poisonous daydreams.

III

I have seen the emerald castle's cornstalk
suns, its cranes and modernist script *Hosannas*,
shattered glass mosaics and forms of nature
frozen in sunlight.

Here its baking mountain of concrete martyrs
caked in summer guano will never find me.
Here the face of death is a nightmare only,
swimming in darkness.

Barcelona, June 20, 2009

Descansos Negras

Where Judith blushes and withdraws the knife,
where witches levitate and Saturn eats,
where rotting Peter drags his bleeding wife
across the black evacuation streets,

there is a song. A cudgel through the air
to which the felon strums and ancients spoon
their dusty porridge on the basement stair.
A broken dog laments the dying moon

as covered wagons veer from the Colossus,
decamping with the towns of the Plateau.
The toll road's spiked with dirty little crosses
and wails of *Las Canciones del Sordo*.

Museo Nacional del Prado, Madrid
October, 2009

CAFÉ LE VIEUX MONTMARTRE

Outside, the shady Place du Tertre's beset
by plastered easels, hacks, and Coca-Cola
advertisements. Jeanne finds a cassette,
Aristide Bruant Chante à Batignolles!,
slips it in the ancient tape machine
and takes her stool behind the gaudy bar.
The painters paste that old Utrillo scene
around the square as tourists storm Montmartre.

Our Jeanne, perusing *Paris Match* and dying
for a cigarette, looks up to find
two lovers at a sidewalk table vying
for the waiter's eye, hands intertwined,
and taking cell phone photographs. "*Mais oh,
mon Dieu,*" Jeanne fondly moans. "*C'est tout trop beau.*"

Belém

I

Waves in open sunlight break on stone
the same cream color as the taxicabs
that course this western beachhead of Europa.
And at the monastery, yellow caps
and Catholic blazers brazenly postpone
communion with the limestone walls. A trope
of sun ad infinitum in an azure tone

where objects take their course or else are taken.
A twisted shell. A sea-worn pulley made
of wood. A medieval tower beached
in morning glare. The shadowed colonnade
looks out onto a grassy cloister shaken
into permanence, its columns bleached
in clockwork light. No object is forsaken.

II

Pyotr Yurchenko sips his vinho
shaded by an awning and some trees.
His series hung to satisfaction, he
relaxes. Here, the bearded painter sees
a landscape, and of course, it is internal.
He contemplates the wide, immortal sea.
At any rate, the sun is an inferno

burning with the heat of homicide.
The Russian chalks it up to global warming—
any conscious artist would. "Relax,"
he tells himself, a gessoed canvas forming
as it always does across the wide
perspective of his senses. Parallax.
It features, nonetheless, a business side.

Across the street some angled figures lope
along the gabled, single-storey shops,
a vignette from a streetscape by Soutine.
An echo of the shtetl. All the stops
are pulled for our Yurchenko. Every rope
as well. His eyes fall to the magazine
he carried from Berlin: *Abandon Hope*.

III

We are not distracted by a charging
foreground. We are floating through a range
of visions. Lisbon, citrus flower white,
is shifting in its April bed as we arrange
the sky and sea in louvered planes discharging
clouds at the horizon. Aqueous light.
A futurist tableau of tourists barging

through a burnished, elegant *fachada*,
not unlike the prison tower basement
or the cool stairs of the monastery.
A mother swings her toddler through the casement,
step by step a song, "*Escada, escada!*"
mimicking a Latin breviary.
"*'Sca-da,*" sings the baby. "*'Sca-da, 'sca-da!*"

IV

And in the choir, a lone photographer
has set his tripod just beneath a life-
size crucifix. He wants an angle on
the altar. His predicament is rife
with comic allegory—he'd proffer,
unwittingly, a photo-opticon
to laughing or distressed philosopher.

But take a closer look. See how the shank
of broken Christ, contorted, twists away
from the intrusion. How the blind technician
twisting on his apparatus, gray
and balding, is a mirror-image flank
of flesh. The S-curved spine of the magician
panders to the crippling of the clay,

collecting images. Creating liturgy
objective and subjective. Fallen man
has risen on the scaffold of his art,
contrite in nothing, following a plan
laid out in the recorded prophesy
of man. The broken Christ is set apart
in this cathedral. Blank. An effigy.

V

Outside we find the tramcars in a line
and soon we're shunted through a neighborhood
of squares, our passage as precarious
as one would think at longitudes of blood
and alcohol. The street as Byzantine
as Istanbul itself with various
conveyances converging in decline

to where a fado melody is heard.
It's coming from the neoclassical
arcade, the Baixa Pombalina, blue
in shadow. Here is the traditional
lament, the brutal rolling R's, absurd
hermaphroditic voicing. *Resiniero*—
Dona Cão pulling every word

she sings from darkness. Destiny and fate
are elemental to the native form
of song, and her delivery is wild.
A woman beaten by the wind and sun.
And yet her sea green glasses compensate
for loss that she sustained while still a child.
She plays a triangle and holds a plate.

VI

And at O Rossio, a reckoning.
We have the reconstructed fountain square
and pharmacies. The theater of lime
and ornamental doors where seabirds share
the brilliance and the hard remodeling
with a New World emperor who in time
will be remembered as an Old World king

in extremis. The cobblestones converge
on Rua Augusta and flow into the arc
before the grand commercial square. We see
the ocean through the gate. But not the park.
The cold Atlantic churns its steady dirge
in tribute to the angles of the sea,
a vista on which histories submerge

in the mythology and terra cotta
chimneys of the fabled hillside poor.
We see them in the narrow window stringing
laundry. Sleeping in the shadowed door.
They whisper, "*Aqui estamos com nada.*"
We also hear the sea and children singing
in the twilight, "*'Sca-da, 'Sca-da, 'Sca-da*"

Lisbon, April 21, 2010

— 3 —

BEYOND THE GLANCING MOMENT

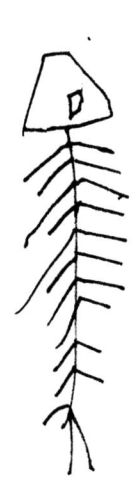

On the Beginning of Constant Memory

In this photograph, Haile Selassie
is pictured mourning beside de Gaulle.
Here is the assassin as a bullet rips through his viscera.
The captions pit "communist" nations against the "free"
under black and white stills from Zapruder's renowned Super 8,
beneath the world-famous mugshot. Under that black swollen eye.

I remember when I
came across the vice president, shocked at the loss he
conveyed. Magazine cameras anticipate
dire proceedings, but, Jesus, the gall!!
And with the blood-spatter Jacqueline still in her free-
fall nightgown. Or on it. Or vice-versa.

Daddy was smoking a Viceroy.
Lucy was singing, and *aye yai yai yai*
had a look at the future, I'd say, in the Radio Free
New Jersey of late November. I could see Lassie
running in circles, no longer saving the day. *Good gal!*
Good Lassie! Sit, Lassie, Stay! She came. I saw. We ate.

Somewhere in the raiment of mourning, we radiate.
I came up like Kodachrome felt on a scout's green visor, a
haircut unbuttered, like the itinerant Gaul
with his blue eyes pleading *Rastafar-I!*
Jah guide and praise in the name of the most I, Selassie.
Jah know me! Jah free

I and I! Leaves turn in the fall. And in Radio(active) Free
Pennsylvania, a river revisits Route 78
to New York. I am there. In the high humble aspect of Haile Selassie
I enter upon the Romantic, an Epoch (*viz* "Era")
of Trial and Error. I
marry and honeymoon 'round Donegal.

And one day I open my eyes in a taxi from Charles de Gaulle
en route to a three star Hotel on La Rue Geoffroy-
Saint-Hilaire. I circle the Eiffel Tower and follow the river to Henri
the Fourth in the Duotone manner of dying at 8
on a cloud-bit Saturday morning in Paris. My driver, Cicero,
stops at the Tuileries carousel. As he

touches the mirror, he brings to mind Haile Selassie, who stood
              with De Gaulle
in a picture in *Life* magazine, the novice *Ra* or *le Roi Soleil*
            sent to free
Babylon. He is eight lions rampant, a chalice and crown
            in the all-seeing eye.

THE DREAM OF ART

The eyes of the Yemeni tribal chief are hard
and wet. An altogether promising start,
despite my painting from a souvenir card
and not from the sitting model. His antique heart
is next. But how can I find it underneath
the robes and leather belt? Behind the knife?
Impossible! Instead I count the teeth
and wait. But I've been waiting half my life.
The telephone rings upstairs. It keeps on ringing
as I adjust the dangling iron lantern.
I'm kneeling in my palette. The lamp keeps swinging,
twirling, brushing light against a pattern
in the gessoed canvas, on the bone-dry size
of cavities and pearls that were his eyes.

*J*UST FRIENDS,

a glistening performance in the Verve
collection, *Bird with Strings*. The famous sax,
a crystal orchestration. Something cracks.
A wing. A cap. The dentist hits a nerve
and all that RKO extravagance
falls back: It's Saturday, I'm in a cab
on Amsterdam and traffic stops. I grab
the jacket of a Sonny Rosencrantz
or Buddy Guildenstern and I'm, like, gone
and gliding off to Central Park again,
around the big museum, naturally.
I pass the bars. But there's a sad refrain
in this arrangement, friend. A dying lawn,
a river, and that reckless melody.

Kids on Bikes

On a painting by David Park

Unreachable. Beyond the glancing moment
when titanium scrapes handlebars
and pinwheels fly against the white cement,
we hear the echoed call. We look for cars

and find the summer's end, and summer's race.
A scramble at the rail that bars abstraction
from a track of ochre clay. A face
and hands, a formal portrait in refraction
caught in an aside. A reverie.
One instant in the long burn of the sun
recalled to orchestrate the harmony
of twilight on an archetype of fun.

An image we regard as an ideal.
A flashpoint in the spinning of a wheel.

Sculpture

*On seeing the cocoons of Judith Ann Scott
and a photo of the artist with her work*

A knotted skein of yarn and Christmas lights
contained the torso. An apostrophe
of swollen limblessness and parasites,
an armature of stolen property
in attic dust. It spoke of motherhood
and would not easily be photographed.
She rolled her heavy eyes. She understood
why sister cried, and why nobody laughed.
It smelled like kitchen towels and Styrofoam,
a bra, a yellow butcher's smock and tin.
It sparkled like the errant chromosome,
or junk if they forgot to plug it in.
And when she pressed up hard against its side,
the lullaby within would come untied.

*American Museum of Visionary Art,
Baltimore, October 3, 2009*

DEAD CATFISH

Persistent crone. Your medieval grin,
(evoking Brueghel) settled in the stone
and switchgrass sometime in the summer light
and stayed. The wind refused to throw you back.
The storm last week could not produce the waves
to reach you where you rotted in the shade

and petrified. I recognize this shade
of gray as semi-permanent, your grin,
the rictus in a fevered dream that waves
and floats, as something of a childhood touchstone:
Once a bird, your image filters back
a catfish. Sick hallucinations light

such dreams in much the way that sunlight
draws your shadow where I step. A nightshade
in the day, you cultivate a switchback
atmosphere, a counter-Lohengrin
where hero is enchanter. Where the stone-
cracked stage shall have no magic swan or waves

of celebrants or swords, but tidal waves
of stagnant air; a concrete satellite
in static orbit fixed upon a stone;
a brittle plinth and monument to schaden-
freude. A luckless path. But here's that grin
and mockery of Cheshire Cat! A back-

and-forth along the frissoned razorback
of clowning time, you have the nerve to wave
me down and hold me here, to press your grin
into the mirror of the lakeblue light.
My eyes and yours, behind their carbon shade
of hardened death, are locked like mason's stone

as viral memory corrodes to breakstone
beach. The progress of your broken back
is mimicked in the cloudline where the shade
of crawling afternoon traverses waves
now audible and focuses the light
remaining on your curtain call. You grin

your bottom-feeder grin of stone, inert
and elegant, enlightened, coming back
to life in waves of shade across the dirt.

UNGEMALTE BILDER

On the "unpainted pictures" of
Emil Nolde, degenerate artist.

Lovers touch and disappear
in watercolors. Cavalier
romantics lurk in purple shade
and yellow flowers come unmade
on Seebüll's coast where evening clouds
play host to lords in trailing shrouds
and closet drawers. Paper fossils.
Magi, circus girls, apostles,
curl together in the dark
as dogs in birchwood shadows bark
outside the master's door. At night
he holds one picture to the light:
Blumen Frau mit Vier Gestalten,
crimson, gold—*an ungemalten*
talisman of German doubt.
He prays and blows the candle out.

Schleswig-Holstein, Germany
1938-1945

Cologne

One springtime morning in Cologne,
on business, traveling alone
and walking at an early hour,
I came on Konrad Adenauer.
Copper-cast to human scale,
a statue on a flower trail
that ringed the chapel of a church,
he stood beneath a newgreen birch,
a solid man. He looked at me
or over me—at Germany
he cast a solemn gaze. Or grim.
For no one seemed to notice him
  save one of little consequence,
    a stranger in the present tense

like S.T. Coleridge in the past
who walked through rolling shadows cast
beneath the vampire-pocked cathedral,
before this modern tetrahedral
church engaged the student throngs.
Amidst the gargoyles and the gongs
that plague this stinking, stony city,
Coleridge penned a light verse ditty
dark enough to be recited
in a netherworld benighted,
or in a perfumed ivory tower,
or to Konrad Adenauer
  on the dark paths of the Rhine
    where foul air strokes the *Sonnenschein*.

Sappho's Letter to Sophie

After Picasso's Figures on the Beach, *1931*

Darling, since our meeting in Acapulco
I'm a wreck. Your coconut-buttered shoulders,
cockled braids, and Louis Vuitton bikini
cover my action

even now! Our Mexican beach encounter
come and gone a year and a half, I'm dying,
lying here, unable to focus, Sophie.
Throw me a lifeline!

No alarm, no casual titillation
pulls me up, engages my soul. I'm even
sleeping through my fiancé's charm offensive.
None of it matters.

Only you, the woman who brushed against me.
You, my fatal island predestination,
rubbed in salt, tequila, and brushing palms of
coconut butter.

ZUIDERKERK

Determined blondes on bicycles careen
across the drawbridge in a steady reel
at Staalstraat, clattering and beautiful.
A daisy chain of fleeting bells, they ring
in transient perfume beneath the clouds
and clanging Zuiderkerk as sunset lights
the summer trees like paper lamps. Arrays
of seabirds circle over Amsterdam
aloft on evening's song. And here I stand
against the rail in blissful vertigo,
above the mirror flow of the canal
where sunlight jumps and swims. Before the fall,
before the northern night, a heron cries
and tilts its wings on landing in the green
and crystal-laden stream of everything.

Amsterdam, June 28, 2007

Rise

And in the morning, you get lots of light.
It pours in from the window by the bed.
There is a burning veil of superfluid light,
a falling sheet of air and dust and light
on which to vet the outlines of your dreams
before you can forget them. It is the light
of day. You take your bearings in a light
so true to objects in the cluttered room
that you are given hardly any room
to hide. You are enraptured in the light
and cast forever downward. Better rise.
The only prayer for darkness is to rise

and paint it white, to hear the blackbird rise
and shake its broken wing against the light
of darkness. A throaty prerecorded "*Rise*"
inscribed in silicon or vinyl: "*Rise!*"
where, in the maelstrom of your tousled bed,
you countenance the old commandment: *Rise!*
One day a dream will end and all shall rise,
a universal dream that holds all dreams
and ties all dreamers to the dream of dreams.
And it will end. And everyone shall rise
and come into a vast cerulean room.
But now, the universe is in your room.

And every corner of the waking room
turns over in the ricocheting "*Rise!*",
enfolding books and boxes, making room
for daylight, an intrusion needing room
to breathe. There is a monster in the light,
inanimate as dread, it fills the room
with something measured in the terms of room

and weight, in quantity and quality, in bed
and floor and ceiling. Light moves in the bed
and corners you. It moves across the room
erasing time and your vestigial dreams.
It leaves you at the mercy of your dreams

as they recede in burning dust, your dreams
that spin in turmoil through the white-lit room,
a foreign language or genetic code. The dreams
that turn into your ghost, the white-lit dreams
that twirl and disappear. None shall rise,
though some repeat on you, the vacant dreams
that circle back like warm, familiar dreams
and leave you with no consciousness, no light
and dark, no narrative, no end of light.
A hole transpires and breathes the dust of dreams
against the window, there above your bed,
as you lie heavy, paralyzed in bed,

the bleak diurnal comfort of your bed,
your legs unliftable, your arms, your dreams
held down against the white sheets on the bed,
the devil sitting on your chest. A bed
is highly metaphorical, your room
a symbol of the grave. Perhaps the bed
is something like a whaleboat on a bed
of blue where spouting monsters rise
and fall. Is it a whale on which you rise,
entangled with your dreaded foe? Your bed
is likely more an island in the light
emerging from the darkness into light.

And in the morning, you have lots of light.
It pours in from the window by the bed,
the window that erases half your dreams
and spins them in the tumult of your room.
Your only prayer for darkness is to rise.

— 4 —

THE BIG MONOPOLY

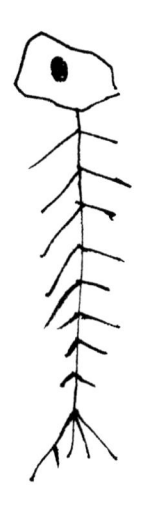

If What You Want Is Fire

If what you want is fire, what you need
is wood. The chemical reaction bit
you have! The very world has gone to seed

and all of it awaits your match. Indeed,
the universe is waiting to be lit.
If what you want is fire, what you need

is air. So tap the throttle. Let it bleed.
Be ready for the atom to get split.
You have the very world! It's gone to seed,

but that means all the radicals are freed.
And that means no one really gives a shit.
If what you want is fire, what you need

is time to burn, to pray the Goner's Creed,
the red ink math and promise on that chit
you have. The very world has gone to seed

and all you hold is sulfur. You can feed
that to the fodder at the bottom of the pit.
If what you want is fire, what you need
you have. The very world has gone to seed.

THE POSTMODERN PROMETHEUS

In my nostalgic alchemy, these things
exchange dispersive properties for weight.
The liquid elements of love and hate
evaporate and leave discursive rings.

You'll find my enigmatic gardening
more interesting from an aeroplane.
That wan varietal, the Hucklebane,
seen circled in a heart that's hardening.

The kitchen of my empathy's on fire.
Its atmosphere a carbon thunderhead,
my range a galaxy of gaseous blue.

The corpse of my devotion is undead,
conspiring with the ghost of my desire
to cast a Golden Idol. Something new.

PERMANENT LUNCH

The nanotech adhesive in the paste
of peanuts pulverized in peanut oil
might give the guy in R&D a taste
of his own medicine. For he who'd spoil
the staple condiment with tiny glues
designed to boost surfactance in the spread
may gain the world in SKUs but lose
his soul between the jelly and the bread.

The Princeton Lab

They closed the Princeton paranormal lab.
Its data had become a sacred cow,
And peer review was screwy anyhow.
They pulled the plug. There'll be no further stab

At reading Sister's mind or fixing dice—
The midnight curveball breakthrough, nevermore.
They closed the Princeton lab, but not before
Assuring the adoption of its mice.

UNDER GLASS

Mythology has reached a sorry pass
when "-ologists" start bringing out their dead.
The Coelacanth is burping under glass

expressing common bottom-feeder gas,
and look at this—a Chupacabra head.
Mythology has reached a sorry pass.

Leviathan? That looks more like a bass—
a large mouth cast in aldehydes and lead.
The Coelacanth is burping under glass

and Chupacabra's coming off bad-ass,
a Mexican *vampiro*. But its dread
mythology has reached a sorry pass—

let's call it phylum *Pitbullshiticass*
or just forget its legacy instead.
The Coelacanth is burping under glass

unlikely in the future to harass
our dreams. And Draculito has been bled.
Mythology has reached a sorry pass
when Coelacanth is burping under glass.

Glitch

Another billion-dollar deal, contingent
on developmental milestones.

A databank on antibody clones,
a hall of screening stations with a stringent

protocol and up-to-date robotics.
Untraceable reagents scent the halo

of a laptop notebook's cryptic semiotics
blinking on the bench where Jane Argüello

contemplates a painless suicide.
But only for a moment. Just a blink.

She drops another sample on a slide
and lays her pipette gently in the sink.

The afternoon recycles with the night.
A synapse scans in cool fluorescent light.

Wheatfield with Crows

The qualms arise. Was it the alcohol,
exposure to the sun, or something worse?
Or was he overwhelmed by beauty's power?
I mean *truly* overwhelmed, unable
to express his feelings, lost with all
his paint and brushes. Did the mistral curse
him in the field, or was the gunshot hour
prescribed by stars, by cards upon a table?

Who really knows? And what is there to say?
Too much, it seems: The calculus of clouds,
the spreadsheets pinned to comments in a letter
to his brother. A pattern to his fits and fainting
published in *Psychology Today*
is said to explicate the knitted shrouds
of crows. But didn't Vincent knit a sweater
of the bastards, painting after painting?

In the Killer's Studio

More penitent than painter, he advanced
through serial catastrophes, a knife
held somehow in the hand that held the brush.
An hour's work was just as often lanced
as was the moment's stroke, the picture rife
with bleeding undertones, an oil gush
of venal violet seeping into black.
He stalked the image like a madman, like
a sulfur-breathing monster on the heath.
On seeing what he'd done—on stepping back
against the table—he would curse and strike
with color at the colors underneath.
The world beyond the canvas edge went dark.
In fact the canvas held the universe
inside a cave of earthy ochre crust
and rags and crumpled tubes. A stark
environment. A crime scene in reverse.
A hedge against the darkness and the dust.

Chance

There was no excuse for our behavior.
Coked-up on the Parkway, downing beers
like assholes. Hell-bent for Atlantic City.
Empties rode the dashboard where a Savior
might have stood. We sped beyond our fears,
beyond belief, unfit for love or pity
to that decimated Sodom on the boardwalk.
Passing all the buses from Gomorrah
we made legendary time and dropped.

There is a hotel on Vermont that I don't talk
about. The big Monopoly, *Tomorrow*,
was upon us and the sun burned till it popped.
Forget the night before the morning after.
Forget the Monday bowline on the rafter.

Landing

He wakes on the wing of a flying fortress,
or something more like a flying favela,
his airship a pile of jury-rigged hovels,
a neighborhood torn in the winding-down war.

It is like that moment when the lights come up
and the plastic window shades seem to slide
at once and the drone of the dream
becomes engines in the sunlight
over Europe's clouds and fields and sea.

There is radio contact. No guarantee
of safe landing, just the voice of the brave girl
on the ground, telling him to ascend the upcoming
ridge and find an airstrip on the other side.

He is confident. Inexplicably in control, lashed
to the ramshackle wing. Low enough, he converses
with farm boys abroad in the hillside village.
Partisans. Their hero, he smiles in assurance
as a wind draft lifts his ship to the tree-cracked crest.

And soon it's his old crew—navigator, tail gunner,
turret-, and bombardier—running celebratory patterns
beneath his hectic descent,
preparing to carry him with his tripod and props
to where they will stand on a whim
at the old revolutionary graveyard.

Lorelei

All last night, I slipped into falling moonlight,
slipped and fell where tentacled constellations
stirred the air. A strangely oppressive sweetness
buried my dreaming

far beneath the coelacanth's endless shadow.
Monsters brushed beside me in trains of blindness,
throbbed their snaking covenant. Phosphorescent
grimaces tangled,

burning candles dangled on wild antennae.
Still the darkness, liquid and flowing slowly,
choked the moss and animal life about me
drowning my senses,

all but one. The song never ended. Rhythms
pulsed, atonal melodies chimed. I heard her
moaning, heard the davening spirit fishes
bidding me follow.

Now in cotton sails I am tossed and rolling,
lost to night's indelible teasing banter.
Breathing clouds advance, and a rapid warming
marks her arrival,

goddess white astride the mosaic harbor,
holding heavy night in her folds of silver.
Waves arise. Viridian mirrors break like
thunder this morning.

THE STRAND

And somewhere on this beach, a single shell
that curls into the soft mold of your hand
might hold the story in its purling well,

might kiss the wet whorls of the ear and tell.
The answer may be spilling in the sand,
and somewhere on this beach. A single shell

in which the winter sky and ocean swell
to mix amidst the millions, scallop-fanned,
might hold the story in its purling well

untold, or spell it to its clientele
of herring gulls. A windy contraband.
And somewhere on this beach, a single shell

recumbent in the clacking citadel,
a china staircase winding where you stand,
might hold the story in its purling well

of untolled memories. A keening knell
unloads the tide and scrolls across the strand.
And somewhere on this beach, a single shell
might hold the story in its purling well.

Books by Dos Madres Press

Mary Margaret Alvarado - *Hey Folly* (2013)
Jennifer Arin - *Ways We Hold* (2012)
Michael Autrey - *From The Genre Of Silence* (2008)
Paul Bray - *Things Past and Things to Come* (2006), *Terrible Woods* (2008)
Jon Curley - *New Shadows* (2009), *Angles of Incidents* (2012)
Sara Dailey - *Earlier Lives* (2012)
Richard Darabaner - *Plaint* (2012)
Deborah Diemont - *Wanderer* (2009), *Diverting Angels* (2012)
Joseph Donahue - *The Copper Scroll* (2007)
Annie Finch - *Home Birth* (2004)
Norman Finkelstein - *An Assembly* (2004), *Scribe* (2009)
Gerry Grubbs - *Still Life* (2005), *Girls in Bright Dresses Dancing* (2010)
Ruth D. Handel - *Tugboat Warrior* (2013)
Richard Hague - *Burst, Poems Quickly* (2004),
    During The Recent Extinctions (2012)
Pauletta Hansel - *First Person* (2007), *What I Did There* (2011)
Michael Heller - *A Look at the Door with the Hinges Off* (2006),
    Earth and Cave (2006)
Michael Henson - *The Tao of Longing & The Body Geographic* (2010)
R. Nemo Hill - *When Men Bow Down* (2012)
W. Nick Hill - *And We'd Understand Crows Laughing* (2012)
Eric Hoffman - *Life At Braintree* (2008), *The American Eye* (2011)
James Hogan - *Rue St. Jacques* (2005)
Keith Holyoak - *My Minotaur* (2010), *Foreigner* (2012)
David M. Katz - *Claims of Home* (2011)
Burt Kimmelman - *There Are Words* (2007), *The Way We Live* (2011)
Pamela L. Laskin - *Plagiarist* (2012)
Richard Luftig - *Off The Map* (2006)
Austin MacRae - *The Organ Builder* (2012)
J. Morris - *The Musician, Approaching Sleep* (2006)

Rick Mullin - *Soutine* (2012)
Robert Murphy - *Not For You Alone* (2004), *Life in the Ordovician* (2007),
    From Behind The Blind (2013)
Pam O'Brien - *The Answer To Each Is The Same* (2012)
Peter O'Leary - *A Mystical Theology of the Limbic Fissure* (2005)
Bea Opengart - *In The Land* (2011)
David A. Petreman - *Candlelight in Quintero - bilingual edition* (2011)
Paul Pines - *Reflections in a Smoking Mirror* (2011)
David Schloss - *Behind the Eyes* (2005)
William Schickel - *What A Woman* (2007)
Lianne Spidel & Anne Loveland - *Pairings* (2012)
Murray Shugars - *Songs My Mother Never Taught Me* (2011)
Nathan Swartzendruber - *Opaque Projectionist* (2009)
Jean Syed - *Sonnets* (2009)
Madeline Tiger - *The Atheist's Prayer* (2010), *From the Viewing Stand* (2011)
James Tolan - *Red Walls* (2011)
Henry Weinfield - *The Tears of the Muses* (2005),
    Without Mythologies (2008), *A Wandering Aramaean* (2012)
Donald Wellman - *A North Atlantic Wall* (2010),
    The Cranberry Island Series (2012)
Anne Whitehouse - *The Refrain* (2012)
Martin Willetts Jr. - *Secrets No One Must Talk About* (2011)
Tyrone Williams - *Futures, Elections* (2004), *Adventures of Pi* (2011)

www.dosmadres.com